Will I Go Postal?

Will I Go Postal?

Sandra Heart

Library of Congress Control Number: 2010906667
ISBN: Hardcover   978-1-4500-7773-6
              Softcover   978-1-4500-7772-9
              Ebook   978-1-4500-7774-3

This book was printed in the United States of America.

To order additional copies of this book, contact:
Xlibris Corporation
1-888-795-4274
www.Xlibris.com
Orders@Xlibris.com
78437

To my mother and father. If you had not been there as an inspiration, I do not know where I would be. Thanks to my husband who encouraged me. Thanks to my sons who also believed in me. Thanks to my aunt Dorothy whose unconditional love and support for me made me go forward with this book. Thanks to a host of relatives and good, supportive friends. Most of all, I give honor to my lord and savior, Jesus Christ.

In this book you will see the words *dogg*, *ex-dogg*, and *female-dogg*. It is just a way of expressing a person who does things and doesn't care whose feelings he or she steps on. I am not speaking of an animal. Some words that some people have spoken toward me were added with them lashing out at me. So please! Do not hold it against me.

Preface

To the postal employees who can relate—you must continue in good faith, trusting and believing that God will bring you through every situation. Some of you that don't work at the postal service but have gone through some similar situations on other jobs can relate too! Your attitude makes a lot of difference in any situation. It is good wisdom to take the time to evaluate a situation. How you respond to a person's bad behavior makes a difference. Of course, I am not saying that I have arrived at that level. I am still growing in grace. Let's see if you would go postal after reading this story! Should I, or would you?

Sandra Heart—born in 1950s in the city of Detroit, the west side. I decided to write this story because I felt the need to let people in on a personal basis, concerning some of the things that went on outside and inside the post office. This book was written years ago, but it's covering so many years. It was not written 'cause you could possibly get fired for certain information released. I feel like too many people have been hurt mentally, emotionally, and physically to receive such a hard treatment from some in authority. Also, the union wasn't always helpful in different matters. I understand that some employees are wrong, concerning different cases. The union did some individuals wrong that were right! Some that weren't doing a good job in decision making for employees had to be voted out, which I did not discuss in the book. I have so much more to talk about but not in the book. Some did pretty much what he or she decided on with management or supervisor, the employee not having a choice to say what's agreed upon all the time. In some cases, you may lose out, they say, if you do not agree. It seems like some union members get tired of fighting for employees, but they want their union dues.

People think about making money, which is good. To what extent should we yield for money and value for a life of an individual's stability to maintain emotionally, mentally, and physically? Some people mentally can't handle the pressure that comes from a job. Some people are without a job for a different reason. Homeless people are people too! Some become homeless for different reasons. Some people have gotten fired from their jobs 'cause of themselves. Some I wonder about because of attitudes of people in authority. Some decide to build some stuff to make a paper trail on a good working individual for different reasons. A weak supervisor is too scared to stand up for what is right! If management says to a particular supervisor, "I want you to give disciplinary action to that person," they are just not being productive. That person has been working very good all day. She is a good worker. Management decides to do a walk-through and pick you out. You pause for a moment with mail in your hand, getting it in position to case mail. Imagine sitting on a stool all day with one foot down on floor and one on the footrest under the seat. Did you know that I felt I was in a prison with wardens, standing over me every day, breathing on my neck? Do you know I have seen mail that was hidden? It should have been taken out for delivery.

Over the Christmas holiday, someone showed me a card that had sixty dollars in it. I said to her, "Write down the address and send a letter to them. Let them know the money was torn through the machine." I added, "You do not know how bad that person needed that money. Never send cash through the mail." She did not want to get involved. I do not know what she did with it. I saw a letter one time that was supposed to be mailed out a year ago. I showed the supervisor. She took it, and the shock that was on her face was unbelievable. It was for someone in the armed service. She might not have even mailed the letter. I should have gone on and mailed it myself. Mail was on color code. Whatever color for that day of the week had to go. The color that is late has to go first. Late mail was still present, and it was time for everybody to get off work. So that color-late slip was taken off. The supervisor put another one on so management would not know it's late. They did not want to get in trouble. They wanted to keep their position at any cost. When some employees did not want to stay for overtime, they hid the mail. Back to sitting on that stool. You don't want to fall off the stool. If you do, that it is your fault. She just paused for a few seconds. Management was not there to see all the hard work you've done. But the supervisor knew. It went like this a lot of time. Either supervisor may get discipline for not doing it, or guess what? You will get disciplinary action for your good, productive work. People have families, sick parents, and children too! Some people, managers, supervisors, and employees need to act accordingly on an individual basis. Stop playing favorites, and keep personal feelings out of the way. He or she may be interested in a certain employee for their own selfish reasons. Because he or she feels that way, favoritism gets in the way of disciplinary action sometimes. I am speaking to those that are in authority that are sneaking around with different employees or getting your chest sucked out because of a position. Why is it that some of you feel the need to sleep around or step on people to move up the ladder in the workforce? Also, I personally believe having respect for yourself, and what you stand for means a lot more in life. Consider people who work hard and have personal problems too! I know there's only so much you can do. But some do not care about others at all. They feel it's about me, myself, and I. This type of person is thinking about the almighty dollar. He or she is thinking about climbing the ladder at any cost, which makes them decide to be mean to good workers. The decision is then made to step on every head of an individual, like walking down a block. This kind of person wants to keep you under their feet and under their control, sinking an individual deeper and deeper in quicksand until they are buried underneath to get to where they want to be. I do not care if that is your girl or your boy as you call it. Some in positions of authority do know about having morals. Some employees know about having morals too! I realize that people have different personal problems that may even affect their jobs. But to harass an individual because you want to climb the ladder should not be over money. Some of those individuals in authority cause some problems for employees unnecessarily.

There was a supervisor I worked for that made me sit in a certain area just to come to talk nasty, lustful things to me. I was scared at that time to say anything. I had just had gotten the job. I had only been on the job almost a year. It was on the second floor of the mail processing side toward the back of the building. I got enough strength to start writing down dates and times. I was tired of being scared and hearing that mess. I have seen him make people's lives miserable. One day I had to get my assignment from him again. He put me again in the same area. It would always be near his desk. Here he comes again, saying stuff like, "I bet sex with you would be real good." I got mad this time. I said, "I have been writing down the dates and the time. If you keep saying those things to me, I am going to report you." His wife worked there. Believe me! He did not want any drama like that on the job. His wife is a very kind, compassionate person. She does not deserve to be dragged through the mud because of his actions. I did have respect for her. I did not want the drama I had to go through with him. He had more since I gave him credit for. He did leave me alone. Imagine how many other women went through this situation from a woman or man supervisor. There are a lot of reasons why some people may think about going postal. You take away their pay for no reason, really! But another employee has gotten away clean, who never really works but just shows up for work. Have a heart now! Employees, stop giving other employees a hard time 'cause you do not like them. PITAS means "Put it to a stop." Have a postal heart for the hardness of attitudes to stop. Close the door on postal jockeys! It takes a corporation of prayers all over the world to maintain on any job with different personalities of those in authority and employees. Is going postal the answer?

Will I Go Postal?

People have asked the question several times, Will I go postal? I look at them, and I ask a question also, "Do you expect me to go postal?" Well, that may be answered after I tell them of my story of my personal experience while working at the post office. Well, I started working at the post office in the 1970s. It was very exciting to get a job paying that kind of money. I was twenty years old with two kids. I had to work long hours and overtime too! I said to myself, *Hey! This job is cool.* Oh, I started out on afternoons; then, I got bumped to midnights. It all started out on afternoons and midnights. I am going to start talking about midnight shift. Then I am going to talk some about afternoons. During that time, working on the midnight shift, I had a situation going on with a boyfriend. We went to the same high school. We were still together when I started working. He became very insecure. He was OK before I started working. I was making a nice amount of money than he was or little less than he was making. He started acting really crazy. He started spying on me at my job, trying to see if I was cheating on him. My god! I had just started the job.

One day I got off work. I spotted him in the parking lot that belongs to the postal service. He was just sitting there! I do not know what he wanted to see that night. When he noticed that I saw him, he started laughing. Today you have to have a badge since they restructured the parking system. Anyway, it was easy for anyone to have access to the parking structure. I shouted over to him and said, "Don't you ever come down here spying on me." Well! Him spying was not enough. He decided that he wanted to accuse me anyway. It is known to be said that the person who is doing the accusing sometimes is the one cheating. Of course, we know he is feeling real guilty because he knew what was going on in the car factory job. I found out that he was the one cheating. Just read along the lines. I am going to get back to working on the job. Anyway, a girlfriend of mine—who calls me Sandy instead of Sandra—said to me one day, "Sandy, that old dogg of a man you got is no good." I asked her what she meant. She said, "Do you know that while you are working midnights, he lives with a woman and her kids?" I was like, "What did you say?" She said, "He has been sleeping there every night when you go to work for the longest." She said, "My old man lives around the corner from this woman."

I knew she was telling the truth. She was a real friend. She did not have kids, but she was crazy about my children. She would buy things for them. She said, "Girl, you ought to just run him over with your car." I really felt like doing just that! But I knew it was not the right thing to do. I told her, "I appreciate your friendship. Thank you! My eyes are open now to this dogg." I didn't want to believe it. But I didn't want to be a fool either. So I had him thinking I had to work overtime, when I did not have to work that day. I decided not to let him know when I would get off work early no more. I eventually went on the street she told me for several weeks. My heart beat so hard. I could hardly breathe. I was really hurt when I found out. I wanted to do something to him, but my mind said that I should leave. He gave me a set of his car keys sometime ago. Guess what! I went back that night. I had someone with me. I took what I claim to be our car. He said it was our car. So I took our car and parked it somewhere. He thought it was stolen. How could he think the car was stolen? He gave me a set of keys. He let me drive the car. Whenever I wanted to use his car. I do not know what he told his girlfriend. But I drove the car to work sometimes. Uhm, did he forget I had a set of keys? I don't know how he got to work the next day or how she got around. I just did not care. I realize now that wasn't nice. Well! He was riding her little family in our car. I was not having that! He would let me drive his new silver gray Eldorado. I was so angry. What was I to do now? He would always meet me at my house about 8:00 a.m. He knew I would be home at that time. He came at the same time for the next few weeks. He did tell me somebody stole his car. I responded, "Somebody took your car. I hope you find it." I pretended I didn't know anything. He said, "I know you got my car." "Really! You think I got it." My mind is not thinking about a car. I had to see if he really lived there, and he did. So now it is on. I really mean it! It is on now! I asked him, "Where have you been? I have been calling you from work. I could never catch you at home." He said, "Oh! I would be over to my brother's house every night, hanging out with him." I said, "You are a liar! I know you have been living with a woman while I worked midnights." Oh, I did let him know where the car was. He knew he was wrong, so he did not give me a problem over that. I gave him the other set of keys. I told him, "I found out through a coworker concerning you and your other girlfriend."

I never gave him the name of who told me. I did not want him to cause problems in her life. Her man lives somewhere over in the area. He did not know what to say when I told him I have been by there several nights and mornings. I told him that it was over between me and him. He acted like it wasn't over. He said, "You can never leave me." He sounded really crazy, saying, "You will always be mine as long as you live." He told me that if he can't have me, no one will. I was young at the time. For some reason, I did not pay attention to those words, when I really should have. Women or men should always pay attention to words like those! Those are some very serious words. I found that out later. He did not let it be over. Now I guess he decided to stop seeing the other woman. She must have misplaced her man or lost him somewhere. She decided to contact me when she found out my number. She wanted to know how long we were seeing each other. I told her for four years. I told her I quit him and that she can have him. I did not want him anymore.

I could not believe I was being harassed by another woman over her so-called man. I never believed in making another woman give an account for something her man did. He has to take responsibility for his own actions. The other woman is not responsible for what your man yields to. That's when I think a woman harassing another woman is stupid. I should have been the one really going crazy and acting out of control. She has been with him for a whole year before I found out. Anyway, ladies or gents, you do not harass anyone. Take time to think about the consequences of your actions. Somehow this woman found out where I lived and my phone number. Every time she could not find him, she would call me, harassing me. She would say, "B—, I know he's there with you. I'm going to kill your a—." He wasn't there with me, even though he kept calling and knocking on my door. I kept telling him, "No, it's over." This stalking woman kept calling, so now I'm stalked by two people. This lady knew where I worked too! She told me she was going to shoot me in the head when I come through the doors of the post office to go home. Can you imagine how

I felt? This person knew how I looked and a lot about me. I didn't even know what she looked like. She must have looked in his phone book. I really believe she got it from him or from his brother. That's how she knew where I worked. Remember, I have a job and I got to work while all this is going on.

I went to the police station several times to file complaints. They thought it was just two women fighting over a man, but it was not true. I had put peace bonds on this man to stay away from me. The police were really not interested in my situation. At the time, they felt the situation was really petty to them. I guess, to them, if I get killed, then it will be considered an open case. Oh! But things started happening for them to get involved. This person called my house every day, harassing me. I called the telephone company to put a tracer on the calls. They could never catch the calls. This person had my gas and lights cut off. She knew all my information. The fire department she sent out to my house so often until the fire department started calling me. If it sounded like a fire truck is coming to my house, I would call to let them know I did not call. She made several false alarm calls to the fire department. The police took interest, I assume, because of the false fire department calls. The fire department—I'm just about sure—wanted to file charges against this woman. Also, the light, gas, and telephone company. She would even call and say that she is going to blow up my house. I was so angry; I knew that if I ever saw her it was going to be over 'cause I had children to think about.

Now the police wanted to get involved, but they still didn't have any proof of the false alarm calls. She covered her tracks real well. She would use different pay phones to do this. Really, I believe this woman watches a lot of television. She knew what to do and how to do it. Can you believe all this stuff went on for about a year? I thought different fatal movies were good movies until I was in a real-life movie similar to it. I was not married to this guy. This situation was as real as it could get. I had to think fast. I even kept the lady on the phone to try to tape her threats with a portable tape recorder. Guess what? I had her on tape. I got her just where I want her now. I took the cassette tape to the police station, but they said they could not hear it enough to tell if it is her voice. You are telling me you could not hear it. I believe he walked to the back and told another fellow officer about it. I believe they laughed. I do not believe for one minute that they listened to it. If they did listen, they probably said, "I will just tell her that I cannot hear it. It's just a petty dispute." This tape was given to the police department before the fire department situation. They kept the tape anyway. What they did with it, I don't even know. It just didn't matter to me anymore.

I was hoping that I would see her. I started keeping something in the glove compartment of my car. I am not going to tell you what it was. All I knew was I felt like I had to protect myself and my children. She just thought she was super chick. She just did anything she wanted to do. I really believe she was one to say, "I do it 'cause I can do that." We will see if you can just do that! And she says no one will be able to stop her. She has obviously done this to some other women before. She must have gotten away with it. No charges must have been filed or gone through with the law. I was determined that it's either gonna be her or me that goes down.

My ex-dogg still kept trying to make me stay with him. One day he came over by my grandmother's house. He knew that I went over there a lot to visit my grandmother. He came to my car door, bothering me. I told him to leave me alone. I had my door locked. He tried to pull it open. He should not have done that! I put my car in reverse and back in drive. He had blocked me in with his car so he thought I could go nowhere. I lost it! I took my car. Sorry! I had to hit his car in the back to get away. He was shocked 'cause it was a sunroof Eldorado. I began to pull out. He was holding on to the handle of my car door. I looked through the window. I saw tears coming out of his eyes. You know why. It was the Eldorado. He checked out the back of his car from my driver side. Really! I did not mean to do that, but he has taken me through enough. And I was scared 'cause he just wasn't moving out of my life. Can you believe that this man sometime ago, before all this drama, had unlocked one of my windows? He must have done it when we had a disagreement sometime ago. Well, one day I decided I would go over to my aunt's for a week to get away from the drama. I heard he was looking for me. I was so tired of everything. Now I go back home and guess what? Somebody is sleeping in my bed when I come home. It was not Fancylocks and the three hares. He had a lot nerve for an ex-boyfriend. It was my ex-dogg in my bed. He must have heard my key turn the lock. It was a good thing my children were not with me. He asked me, "Where have you been?" I said, "It is none of your business where I have been." I was like, *Oh no, you didn't try to hit me in my house you invaded.* Wrong woman to try to hit on. I did not know karate, but I knew something. My mother taught me well not to let any man beat on me for any reason. My mom was like, "If anybody hit you, you better try to lay them out." That means you do a total knockout (TKO) with something. I will beat you down with something, especially me. I am the type of person that does not bother anyone unless they bother me. I am a very quiet young lady. I am not his woman. The nerve of this slimeball. I was already going through a lot, mentally dealing with mess on the job. He had caused emotional stress with everything I had to go through, along with the job.

I ran in the kitchen and grabbed a knife to protect myself. I turned around; I was not myself at the time. He tried to hurt me. I had to protect myself. I started trying to cut this person that was in my house unannounced and that tried to jump on me. If he had gotten to me the way he was looking, I would have been dead or beaten real bad. He became really scared and started shedding tears as he tried not to get cut.

He realized he should not have tried to beat me. My baby brother was asleep in another room when all this went on. He woke up. He called my mother immediately. He knew that he would probably be dead if she did not stop me. She came over right away. She wanted me to protect myself, but she did not want me to go to jail. In the meantime, my ex-dogg was crying, scared to death. I was still trying to cut him. He hit me with a chair, trying to protect himself. I was so angry that the chair broke, but I did not feel a thing. I kept coming. I told you when he tried to beat me that I lost it. I was still trying to protect myself in my mind. Now he would not have been crying and scared if he had left me alone. My mother said, "Sandra, put down the knife." I said, "No, Mama, he won't leave me alone. No! Mama, I am gonna kill him. He climbed through my bedroom window, must have had it unlocked for some time. He tried to beat on me, Mama, you know what he put me through, I am going to kill him." In my mind everything would be over if I did that. I was young; I was not thinking about jail. Well, I got cut because that was the only way I would let it go. My mother pulled the knife out of my hand by the handle, and the blade had cut me. I was so angry I did not feel the knife cutting me. I did not have to get stitches 'cause mom was bending my fingers back. While she was doing that, she told him to leave and leave me alone. She knew that I have had just about enough of all this mess. She knew if she didn't get that knife that he is going to get hurt! She trained me in what to do if a man tries to hit me or hurt me. Of course, he got away from the house clean.

I went to the police station again because I had family members that said it wouldn't be the last time he came over. I'm frustrated now! What is it going to take? Me getting killed to get rid of this guy? He gets my number somehow even if I got it changed. Who was giving it to him, I do not know. Oh! His ex-female dogg somehow was able to get my number too! When I got it changed, She called and said, "B—, you thought getting your number changed would work. I know someone that works at the telephone company." It didn't do any good to keep getting the number changed; the harassment continued anyway. I'm working my job and going through all this, living in fear of two people now! I didn't have any help from the law. Now I got to deal with crazy-acting coworkers and supervisors harassing me too! The question arrives, Will I go postal? Ask yourself from what you've read so far. What do you think?"

Working long hours, mandatory hours, whenever they say. I could not get the holidays off most of the time to be with my family. If you got some good seniority, you could. Getting harassed about this and that. People that don't want to do their job, cussing you out. You had to take it 'cause if you beat them down, you are going to get fired. There is a bar across the street that people would go to on their lunch hour.

Oh! I will get back to the story of my ex-dogg, but let me tell a little of the postal story too! Anyway, some comeback, acting like they were out to lunch. You know what I mean? Oh! There is a difference. Oh! There was also another bar on another corner. Of course, there had to be a motel on the corner by my job, which was called the Thunderbird Motel.

Well, that's a long story too! I'll talk a little later about that, working on the machines at night. It is a mail-sorting machine called letter sorting machine (LSM). There are several slots in the back of the machine. You have to put the mail into a mail tray. When the tray is full, you change the full trays to an empty one. Now you may work with someone who don't like you or who just do not want work. Some just want the paycheck. If this is the case, they usually let every slot fill up on purpose. And if you are after that person, to go in back to clean out the slots and full trays. You have to work like a dog to pull out all those full trays. Put them on steel cages. Then you have to replace them with empty trays. That mail has to be dispatched. While you do this, the slots have gotten full, all of them. There were probably about one to twenty-four and thirty-nine to fifty-five or more where the mail was keyed to. When the machine makes a certain sound, that means the mail is backed up, whether they did it or not. You are the one that is responsible because you are back there now. When you explain that you just got back there and that the person has been leaving the slots full on purpose because they don't like you, you're still accountable, even when you do your best to clean up their mess; you still get the blame because of some favoritism with some in supervision. Whatever some employees did, it was OK, whether they're wrong or not. And I'm like, wait a minute, something is wrong here. You'll be the one to get written up or harassed if you go to the union. So you deal with the pressure of harassment. You feel like the union, half of the time, was working for management. I even, at different times, felt like going to Equal Opportunity Employment division was a waste of my time. I felt that they worked on management's side too! Some of them were good friends with some managers. You didn't always get a lot of results when you needed it.

Will I go postal? Will I? Still going through a lot of personal matters also while working, my ex-dogg and his ex-female dogg still didn't stop there. He continued to come down to my job, watching me. I did tell someone in security. But they said as long as he is not on the premises, they could not do anything. There was nothing I could do! I have just about given up on the police department. I cannot even get anything done by postal security. They were right because he's not on the premises. He is sitting now in the store parking lot straight across the street from my job. One day he came and knocked on the door, begging me to talk. So I said, "OK, what is it to talk about, and you tell your woman to stop harassing me." I let him talk; I had to take a chance and find a way to put this harassment to an end. If I talked to him, I believed she would do something. Then I can get her. What would you have done? I told you I did not get help from the police. He said that he has told her to leave me alone. He said he is not seeing her. He wanted me back, but I said no. So as we were talking, I heard a noise outside my house. I said to him, "What is that? It sounds like someone is outside, around my house." So he went to take a look. The minute he opened the door, he saw his ex-female dogg with a brick. He hurried up to close the door. But before he could close the door all the way, she threw a brick through the screen door, which had glass at the top. He had just missed the glass from hitting his face as he was trying to close the door in time. He was scared because he could have been blinded by the glass. She hurried up and jumped in the car.

Without thinking, I ran out and got in my car to try to catch her. I lost it then too! I was going to hit that car. Then I was going to beat her until she went to the hospital. I didn't catch her because my house was at the end next to the alley. So she went through the alley, and my car was parked the opposite way. It made her car look like she turned a different direction down the next street. I went up every street, trying to catch her. I had really lost it. I was ready to put an end to all this. I felt like Malcolm X—"by any means necessary," this has got to come to an end. The law had not come through for me at that time. But Martin Luther King Jr. says, "We have to pray and not take the law into our own hands." I was like, well! I didn't pray much then. I did have a praying mother. I felt like I had to try to do something. Of course, later in life I found prayer to be my weapon. I really didn't know Jesus. Again, I called the police. They came out! My ex-dogg had left. He said that he was going to ask her why she did that. I told him, "Don't come back. I mean no more." Of course, he left before the police got here. Why should he stay? He was scared because he knew I had called the police on him.

Guess what! The police took a report. They saw that the glass was broken and the evidence, the brick. Now we have a court date. The police wanted to know if I had any witnesses. I said, "Yes, my ex-dogg that happened to come by, that you all could never do nothing about, happened to be over this way. He saw the whole situation." They told me I could finally file to have him subpoenaed to testify against his ex-female dogg. They have her address now! She did receive court papers. He did too! Now the tables have turned. She is calling me like she has a lot of brains now. She replied, "Please! I don't want to go to jail. I have children." I replied, "You didn't think about that all year while you were taking me through changes over this no-good dogg. I had children too! I'm sorry, we are going to court. You are not going to do another woman like this, if I have anything to say about it." Her grandmother called me. She asked me not to press charges. I said, "Miss, no disrespect to you." I was taught to respect my elders. I spoke to her nicely. I said, "Your granddaughter has taken me through so much. She could have gotten a lot of people hurt. I am going to press charges. I want to make sure she doesn't do this to anyone else." My ex-dogg had the nerve to call and ask me why I had him subpoenaed. I said, "Because you are a witness." He's hollering about "you know I don't like police business." "Did you think I liked bull-scrape business from you and your ex-female dogg?" I said. "You should have thought about all that when you cheated. You caused a situation that definitely was unwanted by me. Show up! Or go to jail yourself." He got scared and said, "I'll be there, I'll testify." You know why he said he will show up too? Come to find out this woman was so crazy, she had him scared. She had flattened his tires. She has hit him with something before. That what his sister-in-law said. She told me he was scared of her. She told me her name was Suzy. I said it's his cheating that got him in the situation. He wanted to make sure that she wasn't going to hurt him.

Well, the time came for everyone to show up for court. I was there, and he showed up, but his ex-female dogg was not there. The attorney had us sign papers. My ex-dogg gave his confession of being a witness to the situation. They put a warrant out for her arrest. I heard she moved out of town. I do not know where. I guess she did not tell where she was moving to. Well, my ex-dogg thought he had done a great thing for me by testifying against her. He wanted to get back together again. Sorry, it's just not happening. Good-bye. I still said no! Now through all this while working on the job too! *Will I Go Postal?* Back to my marvelous drama of a job. As I said before, the Thunderbird Motel was next door. Can you believe that people were going over to the motel on their lunch hour having sex? The prostitutes were meeting some of the guys over there (employees), especially on the days the men or women would get paid. Every payday they used to have an armored truck come out in front of the building so the employees could cash their check if they wanted to. You would have male and female prostitutes. There's no telling what all they sold out of that motel. I am sure drugs too! You know that they were getting high in there too! It really used to make me very uncomfortable, walking past every day at night to go to work. There were times when girlfriends or a wife would show up and say to one of the prostitutes, "If my man or my husband is in there, you better tell him to come out now." One of them did catch their man with a prostitute. She told her, "I'm going to kill you and him."

While all this was going on, I was trying to walk by to go to work and go hit the time clock on time. I thought they were going to start shooting several nights, walking past the motel. I was afraid to walk past to go to work most of the time. They also had homeless people out in front of the post office soliciting until the guard comes out and makes them move. The homeless really did not irritate me. I was concerned about other situations. Oh! They had a room at the motel reserved for some gamblers (some employees). Some people were over there, losing their paychecks too! One lady I worked with on our lunch hour, which I can't mention no name, she said to me, "Girl, you don't go over there on lunch hour with no man." I was like, "What? No! I would never go over there on my lunch hour with no man. You mean to tell me you go right next door to your job?" She replied, "Yes! Girl, just about every night." That lady got paid along with her paycheck, selling herself to men on the job. She didn't have to work at all at the post office if she didn't want to. I was outdone. I didn't even want to be around her anymore because I was not going to be talked into nothing like that nor give that type of impression. It is such a wonder she did not die of some kind of disease. I don't know if she used protection or not. Man, I thought in the hood was bad, but I found out I was going to another hood every day that was almost unbearable for me to have to deal with. I had to pay bills and keep food on the table. Keep clothes on my children's back. I was a single parent trying to take care of my responsibilities. I had to work. Whether the atmosphere was straight or not.

People, people, people. Now ask me again, Will I go postal? Oh! As if that wasn't enough, women, after getting off work or coming to work, were getting jumped on by their man for whatever reason I don't know. Men were too! By their significant other, I guess. Maybe because some of them got busted cheating or left the one they have. Maybe their ex-wife, wife, girlfriend or ex-girlfriend could not accept the breakup. Car windows getting broken, tires stabbed, or car keyed with scratch marks. The security guards drive through every night.

You can make a report. Lots of times, they say. I did not see anything. Some women were getting jumped on while coming from the parking lot to work or leaving work. During this incident, they were being robbed. I believe some unknown character or possibly someone set up by another employee is behind this, you never know. Some people are just wicked. My friend I grew up with was beat in the face and robbed. The man hit her in the face and snatched her purse. Anyway, she was pretty fearful for a while, but she got over it. Thank God he didn't shoot or stab her. At work on a New Year's Eve night. When 12:00 midnight came on, I was on an elevator with a supervisor. He said, "Can I have a New Year's kiss? I said, "No! I remember you said you were married. He said, "So? She is not here. It's only me and you in the elevator." I said, "You forgot! God is in here too!" He immediately apologized. There are some that try to see what you would let them get away with. We were cool. He knew I was not like some of those women he could expect certain things from them.

One day I had to work for one of the women supervisors who was interested in a male employee, who was interested in me. She worked me on some of the hardest jobs every time

I worked for her. Sometimes you may have someone else you may work for. I was working under her supervision. The man she was interested in noticed how hard she would make me work because she liked him. So he would always try to get in my area to work with me. He would do the hard, heavy labor for me. I wasn't even dating the man. She would talk to him a lot, but she heard that he liked me. He tried to talk, but he knew I was not interested. He was very respectful toward me. He asked her why she was treating me the way she was. She said to him and smiled, "I am the supervisor. I can do that! She's going to do whatever I tell her to do. You don't have to like it." As if I was in prison, and she was my warden. The job is called—if I remember—the roundtable on the third floor.

The mail processing side is middle way toward the back of the building, third floor, that I was speaking about. This mail comes down on like an assembly line. You have to keep lifting those trays of mail and dispatch them into these big steel cages until they are full. Now someone putting on that job every day for a while could hurt their back. My friend did give me a back brace. Usually, they would try to have at least two people on the roundtable. She chose me to do it just about every day. Eventually, I got another supervisor. He was very nice to me. As long as I did my job, he did not bother me at all. That was really a surprise to me.

Down through the years, I've had some puffed-up supervisors that had on a badge just to harass. You can be one of their best workers. They would still harass you while someone else that they know is hardly doing anything. He or she gets away free without being harassed. You are a good worker, and then you are the one they write up with disciplinary action. This disciplinary action could be a warning first, seven days off work with no pay, fourteen days off with no pay, or twenty-one to twenty-eight off with no pay. Next, you are fired unless the union can get you back. Because you are a good worker, they want to keep you that way, so they harass you.

Should I go postal? Don't answer that yet! I remember I was off work because I was sick. I was trying to get better, and because I could not do what they wanted me to do, I was harassed just for being on work restrictions. I did ask for work, but they played games back and forth. Because it was not job related, they could tell me. They don't have work for me because I am on restrictions. Some people they liked they gave work to even if it was not job related—"favorites." I remember one time the supervisor had some compassion and wanted me back to work. She said to the manager that she could use me to work within my restrictions. Even some supervisors that believe in God and treating people right became frustrated. One of the managers, who was a woman, she said no work was available even when the supervisor knew it was work for me. Some supervisors and managers that really did not like you knew you might have run out of sick leave. OK! So when you are turned down for work, you go apply for unemployment. Guess what! The personnel department would fight me. They would say I am unable to work. I would have to tell the unemployment office that I can work with restrictions, but I was turned down by the job. Now you have bills that have to be paid. You are about to get put out with your children 'cause they are trying to stop you from receiving money.

I did receive unemployment eventually. The postal office hurried up and found work for me after they found out I was able to receive it. It was what she says that goes, she thought. Some women supervisors, also some men supervisors, can be something else. I call them nit-picking, jealous females. And some of the men are just used to telling a woman what to do, instead of asking in a decent way. Do you know some of the lifting that women had to do were very heavy? If you ask some of the men for help, some would say, "You're getting a paycheck like me." The women got the good jobs, car, and house. These are selfish, bitter men. So you did the best you could. Some people did not want to help you out. Yeah, when we got hired, we knew what was required of us. Who does not want a good job? Men, do not be bitter toward all women because you may have to pay child support. You might have lost a lot through a divorce, but should all women have to pay for it? And, women, 'cause your man left you, or like me, I am not even giving him that kind of attention. I am just a kind person to everyone. Should I have to pay for that, when I was taught to be nice to people?

Some female supervisors, but not all, are something different to work for if they have female issues, if they do not have confidence in themselves. I would rather work for a decent man any day. Oh! Little did I know about trying to make suggestions to better the post office. Well, how would I know? The suggestions I made I gave to some supervisors. I was told that they were good suggestions, and they will give me a copy back after it is signed. Guess what! After I gave it to them, I never received anything back. Now you get rewards if they accept your suggestions. How would I know whether I would be the one to get a reward if I did not receive anything back? There was more than one suggestion that I put in. But I can tell you one of my suggestions manifested, but I didn't have a copy, no proof. I really believe the supervisor was going to turn in my suggestions. I became discouraged. I decided I was not giving any more suggestions.

I got sick on the job one day and had to go to the medical unit. I went and told the supervisor I was not feeling good. She sent me to the medical unit. They asked me what was wrong. I said, "I am feeling dizzy." They took my blood pressure. It was normal. They said I could return to duty. I went back out on the floor. I told the supervisor I was sick. She said, "Go over to injury compensation office and see if you can go home." Well, I had to walk over to the administrative side of the building. I was still feeling dizzy. By the time I got to the office through the door, I was in pain. I was at the office window. I told the secretary I could not stand. I was on my way, falling. She ran through the door, caught me before I fell. She sat me in a chair. She called the medical unit. The secretary told her they need a wheelchair, one for an employee. It was me. The nurse who took my blood pressure came with a wheelchair. She said, "Who needs the wheelchair?" "Her." I was crying; I was in so much pain. I cried all the way out the building. Even when the emergency truck came in and got me. I was crying all the way to the hospital. Yes! They had to call an emergency truck. The nurse was so surprised! 'Cause she was the one that said I could return to duty.

They took different tests. They found out what was going on. They gave me medicine for it. Pills did not help. I was screaming and crying from pain. The doctor came back. He said the pills were not helping. He gave me a shot of morphine. The next time I was back at work, I begged one of my friends, "If I ever get sick again, please! Take me to the hospital, if you can avoid the medical unit." On my job there was a man that said I am supposed to be his wife. We used to just talk about how good God is. All of a sudden, he said I was going to be his wife. I told him, "If God told you that, he surely would have told me too! And he did not say to me that you are my husband." He started coming wherever I worked. Have you ever been to shock city? Welcome to shock city. Well, I was in shock city that this man had taken me to. He started asking different people every day where I was working, as if he was my husband.

This particular day, I was working in the flats cases. Flats are the large envelopes, magazines, and letters of a certain size. He found me on the third floor. I turned around; he was there. He looked at me up and down and said, "Turn all the way around for me." On my job we used knives at that time to cut the bundles of flats open to distribute. He had popped up on me so much, I felt like doing something terrible. I had a battle going on in my mind; I did not know what he would do to me. He laughed and left. A supervisor was told. It was funny to her. She discussed it with different women supervisors; it got around. I had different women that did not like me but liked him. They said, "You should not say those things about him." I had to tell on him. Again he was going from floor to floor, looking for me. He found me in the coffee room on the fourth floor. "Get away from me! Oh my god, what do you want? I told you I am not your wife! Move out of my way!" He had this look in his eyes like he could eat me for dinner. He started looking me up and down like he found his good thing. I was the only one in there getting a cup of coffee. I was about to leave out the room. He blocked the door and started laughing. I moved him out of my way. I told him to leave me alone. I dealt with it the best I could. I knew he was a God-fearing man. He is wanting and waiting for a wife from God. But I could not help the man out in that area. I prayed and prayed for him and me. He was really having a battle with his flesh, of wanting to have a soul mate. This stuff was happening on my job.

I had a woman supervisor at the time. I went to her sincerely with this problem. Before I did, this man would wait on me to get off work. He would follow me up the street to my car. I would tell him to leave me alone. He would laugh and think that it was funny. I got into my car. I started up my car, getting ready to go out of the parking lot. Who's blocking the way out of the lot? He laughed, thinking this was very funny. I shouted, "You better move out of my way!" He just sat laughing, saying, "What are you going to do if I don't? I said, "If you don't, I am going to get out this car. I am going to throw something so you will move." He replied, "You would not do that, would you?" I said, "Try me." I was not going to do that. I had to let him think I was as crazy as he acted. It did not stop there. When I left the lot, I was on my way home. Who happened to be following me? It was Bill again. It scared me. I started driving a little faster to lose him. Well, I lost him. I was not thinking at the time when I picked up a little speed. I was becoming terrified of this man. The next day he continued searching every floor for me. The woman supervisors, when I told them how he was following me, did talk to him. He lied about the situation. He still continued. You might not understand my next move. But I had to do this. I did not want him to lose his job, so I did what I thought was best. I called his pastor. I became desperate for this man to leave me alone. I had to do it in a way where he would not get fired. I knew he believed in God. He just was going through a test and trial. He liked me a whole lot. But I could not stand it. So the pastor's wife said she was going to pray. She told me if he comes near me, to call on Jesus. I did just that! He came, and I said, "Jesus." He was very disturbed by it. He said, "Why are you saying that to me, and why did you call my pastor?" I replied, "Because I told you to leave me alone. I am not your wife." He got tired of me calling on Jesus because of him. He finally left me alone, and God blessed him with a wife. "Should I go postal?" Now, he acted like he had plenty of respect. He acts accordingly now, in order. I tell you, what is a woman to do? She is to pray to the Lord Jesus, constantly asking to be kept in his care. Without the Lord Jesus, I do not know what I would have done.

One day I was working, casing magazines and other big envelopes. They are called flats. I had to case them in three steel cages like with shelves. It had possibly eighteen boxes in each one. Three rolls of six in each roll going down and three boxes across the top. I have one case at the back of me and one on each side of me. I had to get flats out of this U-cart or cart. I had to turn around, put flats in boxes according to the carrier. Some went in the boxes behind me. Also, I placed flat in steels on the sides of me too! Some people felt like I was better than them because I was trying to live a Christian life. Things they were doing, I was not interested in doing. Some of the men down there were making bets on who was going to get me in the bed first. I know because a guy that had respect for me came and told me. I said, "You go tell them that the bet is going to be a losing one." While casing the flats, I had to go to the restroom. I came back and went around the cart to grab mail to start placing in the steel. Guess what! I reached in the cart. To my surprise, someone, while I went to the restroom, put an open *Playboy* magazine in my cart. It had a naked man in it, with the longest you-know-what you do not ever want to see. I felt like I was going to have a heart attack. I hurried in closing the book. I saw different men and women laughing at me. They knew who did it, but no one would tell. I got into it with a lady 'cause I would not go to the bar across the street with them. I worked on the machine with these ladies, keying letters to the carriers. It was my turn to go in the back to clean out the slots. When I came back to relieve a machine operator, someone put a postcard on the ledge of the machine I had to key on. It was a pair of blown-up woman's breasts. I told the supervisor and gave it to him. He laughed and accepted the postcard but did not chastise anyone about it. He just told other supervisors, and they laughed. One particular person out of the group was basically the head of the mess. She decided to pick on me on a particular day for her entertainment. She called me a b—saying, "You think you are better than us." Then, she said, "B—, I know what the f—you need. You need some *man-tel.* She was trying to be real funny, instead of the drink Martel.

She is trying to say I need to have intercourse with a man. I tell you, I felt like I was in high school. I am trying to live a Christian life, so I kept quiet. I was in my twenties. This lady was older than me, in her middle thirties or early forties. They knew I had been abstaining from sex, living a life of holiness. This happened years after I found Christ.

Will I go postal? One day on the job, we had a bomb threat. People were panicking. We could not leave the building 'cause the mail must go on rain, sleet, snow, or bomb threat. Oh! On the day of 9/11, I was working inside the back of the building on Fort Street by the Salvation Army. The Salvation Army was next door. I had on my headset radio cassette player. You can see the Canada bridge out the window where I was casing letters. On the radio it was urgent news. I think I heard that two airplanes had just crashed into the Sierres Towers. I pressed my ear up to my earphones because it had a shortage in the wire part. I did not get shocked by the earphones. I got shocked by that news when I heard it a second time. I always heard that if we had terrorists, the post office would be one of the businesses that would be bombed. My heart started beating fast I could hardly breathe, looking at the Canada bridge. I thought it was getting ready to blow up. People were panicking and wanted to go home. All I knew was they would not let me go home. I do not know if they let anyone go home. If we just walked out, we were told we could get fired. They started blocking off Fort Street from downtown and by the post office area. Loved ones were calling. They were terrified, wanting to know if we were OK. Tell me the truth, do you think I should have gone postal? I did get a chance to call home to let them know I was OK. There is a way out of the building where some employees wanted to go. Well, here's another incident. Listen! Some people just have lustful stuff going on in the body. Could not wait until they get out the building to get busy. You know what I mean? You will be, all right! Oh my god. It's been other places too, but that one is sort of off-limits. This is enough for you to know. There are other things I can say, but I do not want to stereotype no one. Everyone at the PO is not doing all these things. There are people that have good moral character.

Oh, there was a situation at work after the news flash about anthrax. Someone has played a trick on the managers and employees. A person put some white powder on the floor of the post office. People were panicking. They called someone to check it out. It was not anthrax. How sick is that to play a prank like that on us. Did you know it was asbestos in the building. Well, we were told that it was not at first. Then we were told it was. Again, people panicked. We were called to a meeting on the ground floor, I believed. Management said they did find some, but it was not enough to do damage. All I know is that many people have died from cancer or many people have cancer that worked down there. You tell me what you think. I do not know if it is related to the post office. One day a manager heard I was engaged. I was working when she approached me. She said, "I heard you were engaged. Let me see your ring." I extended my hand. I thought she was going to say that's nice. No! She did not. She said, "Umh!" She threw my hand to the side and walked away. She kept her eyes on me. She tried to get some disciplinary action for me for no reason.

Have you ever heard of people dating on the job from the ground floor to the fourth floor? One lady on each floor could be dating the same man and not know it. A few women could know it. Some women do not care. Everything has been sold out of the postal office, from panties to porno. If you wanted to see an X-rated movie, the happenings were in the men's locker room.

Some will say "bring your drink" or "I got you, man." They had a TV with a VHS tape to watch whatever. The women better not bring a TV in there. They better not get caught. They say no selling stuff on the job. Favorites can sell whatever they want to. If you try to sell anything and you are not a favorite, oh! They get greedy for money. They do not like competition, so they tell on you. You could get fired. Guess what! It's your so-called friend that envies 'cause you are making too much money. You are getting over, so I am going to tell. I saw a lady make over five hundred dollars a week selling jewelry inside. Every day she would lay it on the table at lunch time and on break. See, managers like her, and some, I believe, were addicted to jewelry. This employee she gave permission to do it, they had something they wanted. I saw a manager come in the ladies' locker room with the employee laying it all out on the table. She picked what she wanted and owed her on payday. She picked out two hundred and some dollars worth of jewelry. Some employees did not get disciplinary action; they were able to do this because the manager liked them too! You know, one day I went to the restroom. I was not in there a good five to ten minutes. This supervisor was standing outside the bathroom door. She asked me what took me so long. She knew

I had been working. She had to go take some papers to the manager's office. She thought I immediately left when she left, but I did not. I told her I have not been in there long. I said, "I don't have to reveal my restroom business to you."

There is a supervisor working at the post office now. He is one of the kindest men I have gotten to know. He should be rewarded. He has been cussed out by managers for his compassion toward people for years. He is still going through this thing with management today. He is so special with the employees' different trials and troubles. I have seen this man get knocked down with words in front of male and female employees. The manager cussed him out in front of me and other employees, mostly women. Is this a good example to set in front of your employees? I felt so sorry for him. I hope one day he will get a great reward. There are two female supervisors that should be rewarded for their compassion. They were not my only supervisors while working there. I had many different supervisors. Now, back to my ex-dogg. He is just what I said, an ex-dogg. Well, he had a terrible life, I found out. We will get back to that later. This character was a hard one to get rid of. He kept trying for years, even though he had someone else. He could not seem to get me out of his system. Please keep in mind, I am still trying to go to work and spend time with my family. Also, I still have to deal with coworkers and different supervisors. My ex-dogg, I did not hear from for a while. A very little while, because I had moved eventually. Surprise! He found me. He found out my phone number.

This particular day he came over and knocked on my door. I asked who it was. He laughed at me. He said, "You thought you got away from me, didn't you? Now, open this door. I said, "No!" He hit the door real hard with anger. This was one time I heard him sound like that. The voice was a very different voice. I could hear the sound of fury and anger. This person did not like being rejected. The next thing I know is that I heard a sound of a gun being shot. My body was up against the back door. I did not know he had a gun until I heard the shot. I thought I had been shot. My arm was hurting, basically stinging badly. I had my son in my arms. I ran through the house to the front door. He kicked the back door in. I had a chance to open it. This door you could turn this inner lock that will lock it when you close the door. The upper part, when you go out, you have to lock with a key. I did get to lock it from the bottom. I did not have time to use a key. He had to unlock the front door before he could open it to come through. There was a door on the left side of my front door. On the right side of my front door is the basement door. There was a stairway across from my front door and somewhat right in front of the stairway is the door leading to outside. Upstairs are two apartments. When I went through my front door, I opened the door on my left and pushed my body on the basement door on my right, so he would think we went outside. With the strength of God, my body busted down the inner facing of the wooden door perfectly almost. I was able to fit through it. I did put the part that was busted down back in its place, hoping he would not notice that it was busted down. In the meantime, he went through the front door leading outside.

I was praying, whether I knew God or not, for help. I was slowly walking down the steps in the dark, praying and hoping that I do not slip down the stairs. This took place at night. It was pitch-dark going down in that basement. By that time, I heard him come in. He ran upstairs and knocked on this lady's door. She opened her door. I can hear her screaming, saying,

"She is not here. Please! Do not hurt me and my baby. I do not know where she is." I could hear him tell her, "You tell her that I am going to kill her." I hid in that dark closet in the basement. Now, my baby was about three years old at the time. When I ran through the house, I snatched my baby up, running. I had my baby in my arms when I bust through the inner basement door, facing down. All the time I had my baby. I had put him down for a minute. I picked him up, with my hand over his mouth while going in the basement. There were several closets; I just took the first one I could get to. I knew I had to be very, very still and quiet. It was a terrifying situation. I stayed there until I heard the policeman's walkie-talkie. I also heard them ask the lady upstairs if she knew if I had been shot or not. She said she did not know. I was shaking like a leaf. I could hardly breathe. I got enough strength to walk up the steps. I shouted to the officers, "I am OK!" They asked me what happened and to explain to them. There were two officers that were there to take the report. I called my mom and dad. They came over immediately! I left with them. I went the next day to file charges. You're not going to believe this. Me and my mother did not believe this. I guess the officers just took this as a domestic dispute as some other calls they have gotten. *Listen now!* They said they do not have any report of last night's incident. My heart dropped to my feet. My mother and stepdad were fussing and cussing. She and my stepdad saw the officers there. The officers were there when they came over. But there was nothing we could do. The law let me down again. So now I was in another dilemma. He got away clean. I did not hear from him for a while. I am still holding my job. He knows where I work. I am still being tormented by this dogg. The words he spoke sometime ago, "If I can't have you, nobody will" or "You'll always be mine no matter what" is the reason I say—listen very carefully—that when a person threatens you, they just might mean it! As you can see, he meant it! Thank you, Jesus! For protecting me when I did not even know you as a protector. Even in my sicknesses you were there. At the same time, I still went to work. Will I still go postal despite all this that I told you so far? Should I go postal? Well, your question is not answered yet! What do you say? Think about it! Did I, at any time?

Index

www.ingramcontent.com/pod-product-compliance
Lightning Source LLC
Chambersburg PA
CBHW020406290526
45785CB00005B/2455